D1525730

Treading
Water

This is not your practice life.
This is all there is.

Sherry Truitt

ISBN: 9798835132287

Table of Contents

for the Three Musketeers
Bob, Dann and me

treading water

This is not your practice life.
This is all there is.

a. Swimming

to maintain the body erect in the water with the head above the surface, usually by a pumping up-and-down movement of the legs and sometimes the arms

b. Idiom

to make efforts that maintain but do not further one's status, progress, or performance

c. The Reality

when you are from shore and the winds change course, sometimes until you get your bearings, all you can do is tread water

Introduction

"The trouble is, you think you have time."

–Budda

In the winter of 2022, my husband was formally diagnosed with **MSA (Multiple System Atrophy)**. It is a rare neurodegenerative disorder affecting your body's autonomic functions. It is hard to diagnose since many clinical symptoms are also present in those with Parkinson's disease. MSA affects both neurons and glial cells.

That means several areas of the brain are affected, including the cerebellum, the brain's balance and coordination centers, as well as the autonomic nervous system.

To complicate the diagnosis, a five-year-old CT scan after a bicycle accident revealed Bob had an arachnoid cyst deep in the cerebellum.

All I knew, walking out of the neurologist's office that clear cold morning, was that our lives would change in ways not yet imagined. There was a weight on my heart unlike anything I had ever felt before, magnified by the confused look in my husband's eyes.

Yet, all I could say as we drove away was, "Do you want to stop for pancakes?"

Prologue

"Well, it's a marvelous night for a moondance
With the stars up above in your eyes
A fantabulous night to make romance
'Neath the cover of October skies."

—Van Morrison

In the beginning, my plan was to write this little book to sort out my feelings about my husband's diagnosis. I thought it might ameliorate my grief, that I could compartmentalize it and keep living a full regular life.

That's not exactly what happened. The more I wrote, the more I realized what a beautiful life we have lived these past four decades. The more I remembered about the past, the more I realized no matter what the future holds, we have been lucky beyond measure. Those are the good days.

On other days the pain is too big to carry. It's the kind of pain that makes others uncomfortable. It touches the nerve of their own mortality and of those they love. I don't drink, so I cry, and I walk, and I swim as if being underwater will make this all disappear. Mostly, I write.

Times of joy, and sometimes sorrow, are how we mark the decades. I thought we would have more decades. In all the dreams I dreamed, I never once thought they would be cut short. As much as I plan, I had not planned for this.

Bob has never said, "Why me?" and I have never said, "Why us?" But in the evening, as the skies start to darken and quiet blankets our home, we wonder what tomorrow will bring.

I learned that a *"bucket list"* doesn't have to be grand adventures around the globe. Joy in the smallest of experiences is around every corner.

There is no plan, except to live.

"Promise me you will not spend so much time treading water and trying to keep your head above the waves that you forget, truly forget, how much you have always loved to swim."

—Tyler Knott Gregson

September 1975
When We Met

I transferred to Temple University after completing two years at a bucolic state school in the middle of Pennsylvania countryside. I loved being at the university and in the city of Philadelphia. I spend the time I probably should have been studying, riding the subways, visiting museums and quirky shops, and noshing on bagels and pretzels from sidewalk carts.

I met Bob in October in the elevator of Johnson Hall on the way to the ninth floor. He was quiet and shy the first few times we met. Mostly, I remember he was kind to everyone. He often wore tan corduroy pants that made a 'swish' sound when he walked.

Years later, our son Dann would also wear pants like that. His first-grade teacher loathed that sound, and I remember Dann would wryly ask if I could wash those pants again, so he could wear them twice in the same week. Oh, how we laughed about that.

We fell hard for each other, and fast. Our first date was at a small theater at TUCC, Temple's Center City campus. Bob was a communications major and took a number of his classes there.

Later, he was a graduate assistant at that same campus. The play was about a mad prince called "Subject to Fits." I remember little about the play, but it was on Pearl Harbor Day, and we have always celebrated that anniversary.

Bob was a cyclist, and between classes, he taught me how to ride fearlessly through the city. We rode up and down Broad Street and at midnight through the rolling hills of Fairmount Park. We spent many nights riding our bicycles through the thick, muggy night air to catch a cool breeze in the park and watch the city lights in the distance.

By November, my parents were in the middle of a contentious divorce after twenty-five years of marriage. I leaned on his shoulder for support after dating for only a few months.

"I'm supposed to pick a side," I say.

He says, "Pick *your* side."

This is the guy, I thought. I knew.

Now Bob's disease occupies much space in my head, but thankfully, the memories of our life together are crystal clear. They have been tucked away for years and now come roaring back just when I need them the most.

"When I wake up in the morning, love
And the sunlight hurts my eyes
And something without warning, love
Bears heavy on my mind
Then I look at you
And the world's alright with me
Just one look at you
And I know it's gonna be
A lovely day."

-Bill Withers

March 2020
A Lovely Day

Our son Dann moved to Lawrenceville, New Jersey in the early Spring. His plan was to continue his Ph.D. program in North Jersey and work in Philadelphia, living halfway between. New Jersey may seem small, but it's 150 long highway miles to commute from one end of the state to the other.

COVID threw a wrench into those plans as the world shut down and telecommuting became the norm. As Dann settled into working at home, we took the forty-minute ride to join him for lunch. He told us about a partially wooded path that circumnavigated his complex. It sounded like a great place for an afternoon walk.

We meandered on the path, following its twisty curves around the grounds. Dann and I were talking as we walked, but Bob kept falling behind. I first thought he was tired from the drive or morning swim, but those were things he regularly did.

He seemed a little unsteady, even though the path was flat concrete. The cognitive part of my brain kept making excuses, but instinctively, deep inside, I knew something was amiss. I pushed those thoughts away as quickly as they came to deal with another time.

I remember thinking, *not today. Today is so lovely, not today.*

"Trust yourself. You know more than you think you do."

–Benjamin Spock

October 2021
The Medical Treadmill
Part 1

Last fall, Bob's primary care physician retired after forty years, and the practice he founded was shuttered. It was not only difficult to start over with someone new, but he was experiencing symptoms that a new provider might attribute to normal aging. Only, they were not normal for Bob, and we were both concerned.

Fortunately, he's turned out to not only be a good doctor but a really good listener. The early symptoms I noticed were difficulty initiating movement, body stiffness, and increased falls. I'd see him out on the property raking leaves, and he would fall backward, the same as when he stood up from the kitchen table. In the house, he walks slowly, his balance off-kilter, lightly holding dressers and tables and chairs.

We swim year-round. Early mornings in the summer, we swim outside at our local town pool with a fifty and twenty-five-meter pool and in the winter at a local fitness center. Frozen hair and sunburned noses have been an integral part of our life.

As a daily swimmer, Bob's major concern was that he couldn't kick strongly anymore and that it took four extra strokes to get across the pool. He was a member of a summer swim team in his youth, a team swimmer in high school and starting in college through today, a daily swimmer no matter what the season.

Dr. K referred him to a physical therapist at a sports medicine facility. It was clear to her by the second visit that Bob's decline required further assessment before she could provide assistance. She suggested he be evaluated by a neurologist as soon as possible.

Bob came home with the news. I spent the rest of the afternoon knowing that when I called his doctor's office, we would be stepping on the medical test treadmill, not knowing how or when we would ever get off.

The woman who coordinates Bob's care was attentive as I relayed both my concerns and those of the therapist. She said she would speak with his doctor and get a recommendation and an appointment for Bob.

The following week she called with the name of a very well-respected neurologist and an appointment date more than five months in the future. That was the first she could get us, and I just said okay.

We celebrated Thanksgiving, Hanukkah, Christmas and Dann's birthday, enjoying the simple pleasures of family life. Yet, there was a cloud over our heads and a very long wait.

TREADING WATER

Over the next months, I silently noticed some new symptoms. Sometimes Bob would mention odd things, like not being able to write cursive anymore. His voice got softer, and his speech got slower until I could barely hear him shout out the questions on Jeopardy each evening.

During the early part of the day, he was alert and conversant. He was good company on errands but had little interest in our usual walks or hikes. I am an artist, and I work upstairs in my home studio. It is a beautiful light-filled space with seven windows that Bob converted from a dusty old attic. He used to visit me while I worked, but that hasn't happened in a long time. By early afternoon he naps on and off and watches TV. He doesn't say much until dinnertime.

I know that soon I will be going down the rabbit hole of late-night medical research on the internet. I know once I start, it will be hard to stop. Five months is a long time to wait.

*"The doctor may also learn more about
the illness from the way the patient
tells the story than from the story itself."*

–James B. Herrick

February 2022
The Medical Treadmill
Part 2

Glad that the snow has mostly melted, we head east to the neurologist on a bright winter morning. In the latent stage of COVID protocols, there is only one entrance to the long low series of medical offices. We don our masks and head for Dr. Z's office suite on the far end of the building. Bob is now using a cane, and this is the first time I've seen him walk so far with one. It magnifies his unsteady gait.

I sit in the waiting area for this visit, confident Dr. Z already has Bob's medical history. He undergoes a battery of simple clinical tests. By now, I am familiar with the fact that neurodegenerative diseases are mostly diagnosed clinically. There are no definitive tests. But, tests he will have.

In 2017 Bob had a bicycle crash and broke his clavicle for the second time. He passed out in the ambulance and, as a precaution, had a CT scan and other tests. He has another fractured clavicle, the orthopedic resident tells him. It's the same one he

15

fractured in a similar crash years before and is held together with pins and screws. This time he will not need surgery.

Bob later tells me he mentioned the accident and the cyst they found to Dr. Z but had never mentioned it to Dr. K, his new primary care physician. In my mind, I roll my eyes.

Bob comes out of the office, and we are told to wait while the assistant prints out instructions for the battery of tests Dr. Z recommends.

Before we return in six weeks, Dr. Z has ordered blood work and an MRI brain scan without contrast to review cerebellar anatomy and midline brain structures. Additionally, he orders a DaTscan to rule out basal ganglia dysfunction.

The DaTscan (Ioflupane I 123 injection, also known as phenyltropane) is a radiopharmaceutical agent which is injected into a patient's veins in a procedure referred to as SPECT imaging. It is done over the course of six hours. I make a mental note as the assistant hands me the referral to look up this procedure tonight.

We make our way back to the car, Bob closes his eyes, and I head for home.

At dinner, Bob explains the tests he was given in the office. They are rudimentary observational tests that give a neurologist baseline information and guide what tests to order. He also mentions his difficulty kicking in the pool and that the doctor wrote that in his chart.

Late the following evening, I opened Bob's online medical portal to review the summary from Dr. Z. My eyes glaze over with the medical vocabulary with which I am about to become intimately familiar.

Bob has ataxic gait, subtle ocular cerebellar findings, worsening balance, and the development of bradykinesia and dysarthria. I look up the words, and since I am with him all the time, I have noticed it all. The slowness of movement, the unclear articulation of speech and decreased facial expression.

It's the last paragraph in the summary that keeps me up for a few more hours. It is clear that Dr. Z suspects an independent neurodegenerative brain disease affecting cerebellar and basal ganglia structures since bradykinesia is not typically seen in patients with a pure cerebellar process. At the time, I do not know what that means except that clearly, the doctor is leaning toward a diagnosis I don't know anything about.

Let the testing commence.

"Winter, spring, summer or fall,
All you have to do is call
And I'll be there
You've got a friend."

–Carole King

July 2021
Brigantine, New Jersey

We were friends with Susan for almost thirty years. She never married and lived with her sister Nancy in both South Philadelphia and Brigantine. Susan worked with Bob, and soon our families became close.

She came from a large Italian family, the middle child of six children. It's just the three of us, Bob, Danny and me. We call ourselves the *Three Musketeers,* and whenever we visited, they showered love upon us.

We took her brother Jimmy's paddle boat out among the waves. Dann built sand castles with her niece and nephew along the shoreline until the tide washed them out to sea. In the late afternoon, we'd sit at Susan's long kitchen table feasting on ripe tomatoes picked and brought along from our garden and torpedo rolls from Atlantic City Nancy had purchased earlier in the day.

In the evening, hand in hand, Bob and I would take walks by the bay. Dann was content to watch

TV with Susan and Nancy while we spent time alone. Like little strings of lights strung across our patio, the tiniest of memories calm me now. I look for more.

We kept in touch as all the kids went off to college but didn't visit as often. When Susan's parents died, we traveled to the shore for their funerals, but it was a time to pay our respects. There were too many people to really catch up.

In February 2018, shortly after Bob retired, we made a date to visit Susan and Nancy for lunch. We arrived early that Saturday and first spent a little time walking by the bay. I brought along pasta with pesto I made the night before, one of Susan's favorites. Her eldest sister, Kathy, was also visiting. She is a nun and school principal and shares the most interesting stories from her daily life. Susan is quiet that day. I know that sometimes she and Nancy care for her infant nephew, and perhaps, I think, she is tired.

No, not tired, but ill, she writes in a note to me the following week. I don't know yet how painful it is to tell your friends that you are not well, but had I known, I would have hugged her a little harder. It's the last time we see her.

After what her family calls a valiant fight, she dies of ovarian cancer at fifty-nine. There are tributes to her kindness and loving spirit on social media. Bob and I think that we will reconnect with former coworkers and friends at the funeral, but only five show up.

After the mass and service, we stand on the steps of St. Thomas and briefly chat with Susan's sister-in-law, holding her newborn son and the few friends we see. We choose not to go to the burial and head to the car.

Once inside, Bob looks straight at me and says, "I do not want a service." I nod repeatedly. I say nothing.

I drive us to an access road near the beach, and we strip off our church clothes for shorts, have a swig of water and head for the ocean. I am carrying a blanket, and Bob decides to take his cane since the boards to the beach are steep and long. It takes us quite a while to reach the edge of the cool, wet sand. Finally, we sit, have a snack and gaze at the sea. There are tears in our eyes for so many reasons.

A little girl in pigtails with dotted ribbons runs by with a sand pail and waves. We wave back and say hello. We are jolted back to the present and enjoy the rest of the afternoon.

"If you need a friend, I'm sailing right behind
Like a bridge over troubled water I will ease your mind."

–Simon & Garfunkel

March 2022
The Little Red Bridge

I spend a lot of time at the park near our home. I sometimes drive there because I say I am going to the grocery or the post office. But I am not. I feel the urge to go when I have been "stuffing" my feelings and smiling, even when it feels like the world is burning down around me.

Occasionally when I arrive, I sit in the car first and talk on the phone to my son. I am the most honest with him, and he reciprocates. I know how fortunate I am that we have that type of relationship, and I know it starts from a very early age.

Dann was just learning to walk when we adopted him. I spent a lot of time in a *holding pattern* waiting to become a mom, and it was delightful to finally spend so much time outdoors together. In spring and fall, we would go to the park most early afternoons. He'd toddle around the soft edges of the LaCrosse field and play at the small playground dedicated to Michael Landon of Little House on the Prairie fame. Sometimes there would be other toddlers to play with. Sometimes he'd just climb that slide over and over. He enjoyed the climb more than the sliding down.

Our favorite spot in the middle of the park is the little red bridge. It spans a small stream with fast running water and now and then a family of ducks. It is flanked by azaleas on all sides and a weeping willow at the far edge of the stream. The bridge curves gently, the slats spaced just right for small feet. Or so we thought. One morning as we walked that bridge, Dann's sneaker got stuck in the slats.

Finally, we wiggled his foot out of that sneaker. But I knew from the look on his face that we were not leaving without it. A man who had been fishing at the other end of the stream walked up the bridge to lend a hand. He pried that little blue sneaker out with what looked like a giant bottle opener and handed it back to a grateful little boy.

That night at dinner, when Bob said, "What's new, Dann?"

He had something to say. "Papa, I got my foot stuck in the bridge, and the fisherman got it out."

"Tell me more," Bob said, and the story began.

This afternoon, I wandered aimlessly around the same park. It's not a place I walk for speed or exercise. We have an active Jack Russell Terrier, and he is for walks like that. On this blustery day, in the meadow between the ball fields, I see a man flying a neon green box kite. The kite soars and dives in the gusty air, and I follow the colorful tail until the trees between us obscure the view.

I see an elderly couple walking toward me with unsteady gaits. The woman is using her wheelchair as a walker, her husband close beside her. I say hello, and he responds with a small smile, but she is intent on taking small measured steps on the gravel path and does not look up.

I keep walking, knowing I should be heading home. I want to stop at the little red bridge before I hop back in the car. I'm thinking about all the people I've passed on my way today. I'm thinking about the brave faces we wear because showing the truth is sometimes more than we can bear.

When I get to the bridge, it is empty, and I notice small curls of faded red paint flaking in the sun. Eyes closed with the warm sun on my face, I look skyward. I've stood on that bridge countless times over the past thirty years, and now I carry those memories home to my husband and think about what I'm going to make for dinner.

"Never test the depth of river with both feet."

–Warren Buffet

February 2022
The Medical Treadmill
Part 3

The bloodwork work for Cobalamin, C-Reactive Protein and the Sedimentation Rate is easily scheduled. All the results come back in the normal range.

Two weeks later, we head to a Radiology center for the first scheduled MRI. It's an efficient but busy center I came to years ago. When they call Bob's name, we walk to *Window #5 to* fill out paperwork I'm certain I have filled out before. The clerk hands the documents to him, and he slides them to me to fill out. I see his eyes over his mask and know he's just not up to completing those forms.

I keep all of Bob's pertinent information on my phone and quickly fill out the forms, then point to the "x's," and he signs where indicated. I matter-of-factly tell him what he has just signed.

We sit in the two-tiered waiting room until they call for him again. While his MRI is underway, I get fidgety. Loved ones and caregivers sit in the waiting areas glued to their phones. I decide to take a walk on the grounds. There is a day care center adjacent to the parking lot and it's nice to see little ones on the playground.

In the distance, I see a middle school that looks familiar even though we are not near our home. It's where I took Dann years ago to watch his friend Nora in a dance recital. I also took a CPR class in the cafeteria of that school before we brought Dann home. It starts to drizzle, but I have no intention of going back to the waiting room until the last minute.

I put up my umbrella and walk down a driveway assigned to drive through COVID testing. There is a woman in a little kiosk at the far end, and except for the two of us, the road is empty. That's a good sign, I think.

I return to the center just as Bob is escorted out of the testing area, holding a cloth bag with his paper gown and a pair of socks. I smile through my mask and hope he is smiling back. I know now not to ask how he is doing right away. He focuses on one thing at a time, and I am sure he just wants to get out of there. I crook my arm, and he slips his arm in as we walk through the parking lot.

It's a pleasant drive home, even in the rain. We pass by a horse farm with a long low post and rail fence and grassy meadows. Once painted white, the wood has weathered to a silvery gray. There are two horses far in the distance. We talk about how nice it is to see green space in the midst of overdevelopment.

The following morning a scheduler from the Radiology Center phones to schedule Bob's next procedure, a DaT SPEC scan. DaTscan is a drug that is injected into the bloodstream to assess dopamine-containing neurons, which are involved in controlling movement. By analyzing the images, the neurologist can help determine whether the symptoms Bob is experiencing are the result of Parkinsonian syndrome.

During my research, I have seen numerous scans of patients with regular comma-shaped dopamine and tiny spheres of dopamine in Parkinson's patients. But as I said, I have this nagging feeling that Dr. Z suspects something besides Parkinson's Disease. I'm not ready to think about that yet.

Two weeks later, we arrived at the center to begin this test. It's going to be a long day. We check in, and this time, we are directed to the nuclear medicine area of the facility. It feels more serious on this side of the building.

While we are waiting, I ask Bob if he wants me to explain the series of steps for the day. He shakes his head no but doesn't let go of my hand. The nuclear imaging technician comes to escort Bob to the testing area. So it begins, again.

The DaTscan, once started, takes approximately thirty to forty-five minutes. However, following injection of the DaT agent, approximately three hours are required before the agent has achieved appropriate concentration in the brain. One hour before the exam, Bob receives a drug to allow him to safely take the iodine required for the scan.

After the injections, we are told to go home and return after lunch. Dann is working from our house today and taking care of the dog. Dann is a good diversion for Bob and the time passes quickly. It has started to sleet, so we leave early to make it back for the test in time.

They take Bob right away, and I remain in the waiting room because the weather is bad. There are only a few other people in the area. A daughter is explaining to her mom that a camera will be positioned above her, and she must remain *very* still for about thirty minutes while images are taken. She tells her the scanner will be very close to her head but will not touch her. I explained this to Bob a few days earlier, and I hope he remembers when the technician tells him again.

They take the mom across from me. Her daughter looks weary as she slumps back in the chair. She smiles a half-smile, and I'm not sure what to say. I smile back and tell her she did a good job of explaining the procedure to her mom. She confides her mom is in the beginning stages of dementia, and once before, when she had this test, she moved halfway through. They had to repeat the test from the beginning the very next week.

Also in the waiting room is an older gentleman whose wife was tethered to oxygen as she passed me moments before. He senses an opening and begins to share his wife's complicated medical condition. He tells us she needs surgery but has refused, and so they come here every month for tests and a procedure in lieu of the operation. The daughter tells us she had to take a demotion at work to spend more time caring for her mom. She appears to be in her early forties, but her weary, slumped shoulders and tired eyes are of a much older woman.

The chat continues, but no one asks why I am here. I don't think they can bear another story, another sorrow. I want to run, but I stay put. I put my AirPods in after an appropriate amount of time and downloaded a podcast from my phone.

"His eyes were the color of the sand
And the sea
And the more he talked to me, you know
The more he reached me."

–Joni Mitchell

March 2022
"D" Day

Today is "D" Day. We are heading to Dr. Z to discuss the test results and obtain a formal diagnosis. Our care coordinator has called us twice before to let us know the results of the first two tests. The blood work is all in the normal range. The first MRI of the brain showed a retro cerebellar arachnoid cyst and scattered hyperintense T2 lesions. The doctor told her to say neither of these required attention immediately, and he would explain further in a few weeks. There is radio silence about the DaT Scan.

I walk calmly across the parking lot, but my heart is beating out of my chest. I ask Bob if he is nervous, and quietly, in short, clipped sentences, he says no. He tells me he doesn't care what they say it is. Whatever medication the doctor prescribes to help me kick hard and swim stronger, I'll take. He is linearly focused on swimming.

Two years ago, his balance problems forced him to give up riding his bicycle. He had a series of small falls, *road rash*, and the inability to carry his bike down to the basement safely. Next to Dann and me, Bob loves to swim even more than he loves to ride.

Oh, please, I think, *don't take that away from him too.*

I spend way too many hours researching the symptoms on my laptop. I kept another tab open to look up all the words I've heard of but had no idea what they meant. I have read in the doctor's notes in Bob's medical portal that he has some classic parkinsonian symptoms, bradykinesia, but no tremors. It's clear in retrospect that the neurologist's diagnosis is leaning elsewhere.

I go into the exam room with Bob after he gets weighed, and shortly thereafter, Dr. Z comes in dressed remarkably like Bob. He talks for a very long time, at least twenty minutes. I know Bob is not processing most of what he says, and I know it is my responsibility to make sense of it all.

I steady myself and ask pertinent questions, which let the doctor know I am beginning to understand even if Bob does not. I am forever grateful that the Jefferson Health portal is not only shared by all of Bob's physicians but is a living document, a compilation of his entire health history that I can read at any time.

"Your case," Dr. Z begins, "is one in ten million."

He explains Bob's first MRI of the brain showed a retro cerebellar arachnoid cyst. The second brain scan, the nuclear DaT Scan, was abnormal because of a symmetric decrease of uptake in the putamen.

That is the outer part of the lentiform nucleus of the brain.

He looks at Bob and explains that his scan, indicative of basal ganglia dysfunction, is representative of **Multiple System Atrophy of the cerebellar type. (MSA-C)** I gulp because I am not sure what that is exactly. I look over at Bob's sweet blue eyes, soft as an island sea, and he is expressionless. It is clear to me Dr. Z has consulted with other neurologists before coming to this diagnosis.

I know I will be up all night reading about it, but I have to say something so that Bob hears me. I ask the doctor, "So what you suspected at first was Parkinson's Disease, is not, correct?"

He gently answers, "No, it is not." I know at this moment, it is *really* significant, and we will be charting unknown waters.

Dr. Z says in his notes I read a few days later that he explained to the patient (Bob) his clinical impression and counseled him about the disease, which has no specific treatment but only symptomatic treatment.

The notes go on to say he will prescribe a trial of carbidopa/levodopa 25/100 mg half a pill three times a day for a week to increase to one pill three times a day to observe if that would improve bradykinesia. He discusses the side effects and possible benefits of carbidopa/levodopa. He does not think it will help with Bob's loss of balance.

He asks if we have any more questions, and we both say no. Every physician relaying a diagnosis knows patients and their families come armed with some information but are not always equipped to have a sanguine discussion in those early moments.

We briefly chat about physical therapy, but I make no comment on that for now. He offers to talk with us at any time, and I tell him once we discuss the diagnosis. What I really mean is *when I understand what in the world this is*, I will have questions.

I make a follow-up appointment for Bob in three months, and we head down the long corridor and out into the frigid air. I am numb. Over pancakes, I don't ask Bob if he understands what the doctor says, but if he has thought of any questions?

He says, "So, I don't have Parkinson's, but I do have some of the symptoms. And, there's no name for what I have."

Yes, Bob, there is a name for what you have, and when I look up that disease, I'll tell you more. But, before I can even say that, he says, I wonder how long it will take for us to know if the medicine is working. I don't know. I don't know.

"It's no use going back to yesterday,
because I was a different person then."

— Lewis Carroll "Alice's Adventures in Wonderland"

March 2022
Down the Rabbit Hole

We are watching the last episode of *The Marvelous Mrs. Maisel,* and the only thing that registers are the beautiful clothes Midge and Rose wear. I am not following the plot or the dialog, and I hope that Bob will go to sleep as soon as it is over. He does.

I have work to do. I promise myself I will only look at abstracts from Pub Med (pubmed.ncbi.nlm.nih.gov), John Hopkins and perhaps the Multiple System Atrophy Coalition (multiplesystematrophy.org) might suggest.

I'd love a cup of coffee, but it's 10:00 PM, and I think some chamomile tea might be a better choice. While the tea is brewing, I step out onto the porch and the night sky greets me with a blanket of stars. It was a long and arduous journey to bring our son home to America.

One night when he was about three, I was tucking him into bed, and he asked, "Why did it take so long for you and Papa to come get me, Mama?"

It did take a long time, Dann, a very long ten months. What I told him was, I knew it was long, but every night when I looked at the stars in the sky, I knew he was looking at those same stars and that his foster mother would keep him safe until we were allowed to travel to bring him home.

Tonight when I look at the sky, I think about all the families that received news like we did today and how we will never be the same again. I say a prayer for them and for strength, but mostly to practice compassion for the people I will meet along the journey.

I'm proficient at research. It is both a blessing and a curse. One of the ways I worked my way through college was as a social research assistant. I decided that whatever I learned would be divided into two sets of data.

One: A knowledge base for that I can share with Dann. He can read whatever parts he chooses.

Two: A knowledge base is for Bob, and I wrestle with this at the outset.

Even when we thought his disease was something else, he never looked up the symptoms. I prepare some fundamental questions and answers. I am genuinely surprised that he relies on me without question. He doesn't read any of it.

TREADING WATER

Over the decades, I have never had to parse my words with Bob. We pretty much agree politically, spiritually (although raised in different religions), and how we saw our life unfolding. Until now. He still reads the New York Times every day, but when I ask him about a story, he says he mostly just reads the headlines.

We are sitting at the kitchen table playing Wordle after lunch. He keeps forgetting to take his L-Dopa. I use this as an opportunity to explain that protein interferes with its absorption, so the pill must be taken one hour before meals or two hours after. I tell him if he forgets, lunch and dinner will be late. He nods, but the next day still doesn't remember. I don't want to hover, I want Bob to be a responsible participant in his health care, but I don't yet know if I am expecting too much.

One of Bob's care coordinators explains *dual-task cost* to me. I play that over in my mind. In this case, it means a person whose balance is less automatic (and this is a major issue for Bob) must pay more attention while walking and cannot be a good listener. Conversely, if you want to talk about an important topic, it's crucial that your partner is sitting and not engaged in another activity.

I soon put this to a test. We belong to a Cinema Club that was dormant during COVID. The club is run by two film aficionados, and we meet at our public library. Although it was nice to finally be back in person, I was not interested in this month's film. I walk with Bob into the meeting room to say hello and arrange to pick him up after the movie. He sits right away and starts listening to the guys. Mostly I hear them talking to him.

Apparently, there was a lot of health talk before the movie because the next day, Bob asks, "There's no name for what I have, is there?

Oh, yes, Bob, there is. Now, how do I explain it, since you won't read anything. I will be succinct, not give too much information and answer any questions he may have, and if I don't know, we'll call the doctor. This is the first conversation since visiting the neurologist and won't be the last.

I tell Bob that Dr. Z and a team of neurologists have diagnosed him with **Multiple System Atrophy,** or **MSA** for short. Bob has a good knowledge of biology. I tell him that it affects the autonomic nervous system (the part of the nervous system that controls his internal functions such as heartbeat, blood pressure, urination, digestion), the substantia nigra (critical brain region for the production of dopamine) and the cerebellum. I briefly explain that the functions of the cerebellum are maintaining balance, coordinating movement, and vision. He is mentally checking off the symptoms he has.

I ask if I should go on? It's a lot to explain and not get emotional. He nods. I finish up by saying your condition is called **MSA-C.** There are other types. I briefly say his care team is aware his main challenges include ataxic gait and difficulty swimming. He seems to relax when I say this part because right now, that's all he wants them to know.

I stop talking. We eat sliced avocado and tomato on crackers because dinner is going to be late. I am certain Bob understands what I just said, and I hope he will talk a little about how he is feeling. I clearly remember this moment because I have tears in my eyes, and he barely reacts.

Truth be told, although research is deepening medical understanding of MSA and other atypical Parkinsonian type disorders, they are progressive, and there are no treatments that effect a cure.

I am bone tired and fall into bed. Every morning we wake brings new challenges, and I fall asleep without another thought.

"Call any vegetable
And the chances are good
The vegetable will respond to you."

–Frank Zappa

July 1976
Music and Vegetables

It was the summer of the Bicentennial and Philadelphia was crowded and hot. There were thousands of tourists, and we escaped from the city every chance we could.

We listened to a lot of music as we traversed the back roads from Chester County to New Hope and the Jersey Shore. Bob's tastes ran from Emerson, Lake and Palmer and King Crimson to his favorite, Frank Zappa. I did not really know his music, but the year before, my friend Candy and I had stumbled into a movie theater that was showing "200 Motels" in Spanish. It is a mockumentary about the lives of peripatetic rock stars directed by Zappa and also stars Theodore Bikel, Keith Moon and Zappa's band, The Mothers of Invention.

My tastes ran softer. Carole King, James Taylor and Joni Mitchell. Always, Joni Mitchell. Our preferences in music were like a Venn diagram because, in the center, our tastes overlapped. Oh, the beauty in that overlap was magnificent. We both loved Crosby, Stills, Nash and Young, Chick Corea, Dave Brubeck, Miles Davis, George Gershwin and the incomparable Al Jarreau.

One Valentine's Day, many years later, Bob made me a mixed CD of Joni Mitchell songs for my car. I still knew every word, but for the first time, I really listened to the lyrics. While I thought she sang of halcyon days, it was far deeper and captured the zeitgeist of the times.

When Frank Zappa died in 1993, it shook Bob. Bob was thirty-eight, and Frank died at fifty-two. We were married more than a decade by then, had purchased our home and become parents.

It was about the same time that I became a vegetarian. Before we became parents, we worked long hours. We ate on the fly and while we were active, I knew our diet was not the best. We had to set a better example for our son.

I now ran my business from home to be with Dann, and it was easier to prepare healthy meals for us all. It took many more years until I became vegan and then fully plant-based. I felt amazing and used those vegetables like a shield to protect my health. While Bob still ate some animal protein, he also ate my plant-based meals and enjoyed them.

When YouTube became popular, and right up until recently, I subscribed to channels featuring many plant-based chefs, doctors and dieticians. I wonder if any of them know vegans who became very ill? There are even more influencers who tell you how to lose weight and reverse chronic disease by becoming vegan. I will never ever tell someone how or what to eat. I am leaner and stronger, and I know that a plant-based diet is the right thing for me. I do not know if it is right for everyone.

Can it reverse all diseases? This time last year, I would have unequivocally said yes. I am less sure today. I've sifted through copious abstracts from well-respected physicians and researchers. You *can* improve your heart health, lower your cholesterol and visceral fat. I believe vegans will have a lower incidence of both cancer and heart attacks.

My husband's disease is neither hereditary nor situational specific. Like many autonomic diseases, including Parkinson's, MSA and half a dozen others, strike without warning in the prime of life. Though we note subtle changes in our loved ones before they are diagnosed, we cannot stop the progression. And, in these cases, does diet matter?

Every day there are more questions than answers, but what I know for sure is if my husband asks for an ice cream cone, I will make sure he gets one.

"Raise your right hand. Take off that hat. Raise your right hand! Will you take off that hat!"

The Three Stooges

October 2009
The Gray Striped Hat

I hail from the deep south but grew up in Pennsylvania. Even though the winters were frightfully cold and snowy, I never wore a hat. Even when we would build snow forts in the yard and my mittens were crusted with icy bits, my head was bare. By the time I would come into the house, my ears were frozen.

Perhaps that's why I can swim even in the winter. I always wear a hat now, my damp hair peeking out from under and freezing with little ice crystals as I walk through the gym parking lot. Bob, on the other hand, has always worn a gray and cream wool tweed cap as long as I've known him.

When I. Goldberg, the grand army surplus store in Philadelphia, was closing down, we purchased a dozen of them and have since located an online surplus shop. He keeps them in various stages of wear, although the cap he last wore under his bicycle helmet now sits dormant on a peg on our breakfast room wall.

More than a dozen years ago, we got caught in a snowstorm, and Bob placed his warm cap on my head and pulled up his hood. Where has this feeling been all my life? I was hooked.

A few months later, Bob gave me a beautiful cap of my own. It was knit in fine wool with patterned stripes in variegated shades of gray and cream. Near the top was one knit stripe of carnation pink. It was me, and I wore it everywhere.

This next part is a true story, although it will be hard to believe. I lost the cap less than six months later. I looked everywhere for it, but it must have fallen out of my backpack when I was unaware.

In the fall, just as the leaves are turning, we hike one Sunday morning around Hopkins Pond. It is cold and damp where the trees shade the trail. Up in the distance, where the sun peeks through dappled trees, is my hat! It's probably not my hat, but it is exactly the same pattern. I tell Bob it is still warm, although there are no hikers nearby. He puts it on my head, and we pass no one on the trail in either direction.

After our hike, we head up the steep hill between the trail and the parking lot. Bob's truck is the only one there. The hat is mine.

It is only mine for a short time. I am only renting the joy of that hat. Two mornings later, I head down the front steps in the early morning to get the newspaper wearing pajamas and my hat. In that split second, it both starts to rain, and a young man in a wheelchair and his girlfriend are headed to the local high school. I've seen them many times before. She wears a hoodie. His head is bare. I walk swiftly after them and take the hat off my head and put it on his.

He tells me I don't have to do that, I tell him I have others, and he smiles and says thank you.

More than a year has passed. I am picking up Chinese food from Chow's on a busy Friday night. It is before the days of Uber Eats, so Bob drops me off in front, circles the block, and I am out with the food before he returns. My hands are full, and a young woman holds the door open for me. As I say thank you, I notice she is wearing the gray hat with the carnation pink stripe.

"One foot in front of the other.
Repeat as often as necessary to finish."

–Haruki Murakami

April 2022
One Foot In Front of the Other

It is the first time we have seen Bob's primary physician, Dr. K since last October. Bob is sitting on the exam table, and I sit across from him in a soft blue chair. The physician's assistant sits next to me, asks Bob some routine questions and types in the answers. The computer screen is on a large swivel arm, and it shakes when he stands up.

Dr. K comes in and takes the seat next to me. Instead of staring at the computer screen, he greets us, sits down in scrubs that match the chair and smiles.

He looks at Bob and says, "What's going on?"

Bob begins to chronicle the series of events since last October. It's hard for him to articulate through the mask, and he is unsure of the timeline. I am intimately familiar, and he asks me to take over.

I get to the part where Dr. Z suspected Parkinson's, but I say it is not. "Oh, that's good," he says.

"No," I say softly, "it's not."

I tell him the diagnosis is MSA, and I see his shoulders drop, and I see him steady himself before he speaks. It's almost imperceptible, but we are sitting close to each other, and I feel it. I know by this time, less than 0.7 people out of 100,000 are afflicted with MSA, and I know Dr. K is familiar with its symptoms and progression. It's the second time in the last two months I am confronted with both the rarity and severity of this disease.

Now he takes a few moments to view Bob's portal. He reads the notes submitted by Dr. Z, the diagnosis and his recommendations for *next steps* and medications. He concurs. I tell him Bob has just started taking the Carbidopa/ Levodopa. I explain that physical therapy is indicated, and Bob nods, but we did not get a referral yet.

He tells us he'll take care of that today so Bob can get started as soon as possible. Besides therapy to strengthen his leg muscles, he needs assistance with his ataxic gait and ways to figure out how to maintain his balance or to quickly recover when he falls. Dr. K tells us to let him know if we have questions, walks us to reception and says he will see us in a few months.

At reception are the forms we need for Physical Therapy, and I plan to make an appointment as soon as we get home. We make a follow-up appointment with Dr. K and once again head for home.

I fix lunch, and afterward, Bob rests. I take a short walk with the dog, and when I return, the mail has arrived. There's an envelope from the neurologist with the physical therapy authorization inside. I decide to bring both referrals to the first appointment.

We have a choice of two practices and decide to go with the smaller one, closer to home and Bob's physician. Fortunately, there is an appointment available next week. Bob asks that I sit in on the first session.

Once again, we relay Bob's medical history. The timeline gets longer, and I'm glad I can refer to my phone. The physical therapist takes copious notes, listens to our concerns, asks questions and then completes an initial physical evaluation. Bob explains the difficulty he has kicking in the pool.

"Freestyle?" the therapist asks.

Bob answers yes and tells him on his back he is having an easier time. He tells us at the next appointment, he will have a plan for Bob along with a series of exercises he will practice at home. The plan may change depending on what Bob can accomplish, and new challenges will be added weekly. Some will require my assistance.

The office is at the edge of stately homes and a small park over a hill in the distance. I look forward to walking forty minutes twice a week while Bob is working on getting stronger. Even in the early days of illness, a care partner can lose sight of their own health. I promise myself that will not happen.

When we walk through the parking lot, Bob is unsteady and tired. He is hopeful, though, for the first time in months. Finally, there is something concrete he can do that may help him regain some strength.

"I have eaten. the plums. that were in. the icebox. and which. you were probably. saving. for breakfast. Forgive me. they were delicious. so sweet. and so cold."

–William Carlos Williams* from "This is Just to Say"

June 1964
Summers with Sunna

I started spending summers with my Grandma Sunna when I turned nine. My mom was overwhelmed taking care of four small kids, and an arrangement, unbeknownst to me, had been made for me to go to North Jersey. My mom looked sad when she told me, but I was dancing on the inside.

My Grandpa Sam and Sunna came to pick me up the first Saturday after school was over. We lived in Pennsylvania, and the trip to Passaic was over two hours, so as soon as Sam had a cup of coffee, we hit the road. I sat in the back seat of different cars they owned over the next five summers. They were always large, old and roomy gray or green sedans. I bounced around in the back seat in the days before seat belts and inhaled the smell of Sam's cigars. My grandparents were still Orthodox Jews at the time, and even though they drove on the Sabbath, Sam only chewed the end of the cigar. He did not light it.

North Jersey was a very different world for me. My parents' home was on the outskirts of Bethlehem, in a township with well water and neither street lights nor sidewalks. In Passaic there were well-lit sidewalks, and we could walk everywhere. My grandparents lived in a roomy apartment attached to what I remember as a white mansion on the outskirts of town. It was owned by a distant cousin who was a prominent physician in his day. It had an expanse of lawn on all sides and was surrounded by a low black iron fence. The apartment had its own entrance with a wide brick porch, and so to me, it seemed like the house was all ours.

My grandpa worked for Ballantine Beer as a delivery driver and was gone a lot. My grandma never said she was lonely. She only expressed how happy she was to have me with her. Years later, when we talked about those times, she told me she worried about my mom and taking me was the only way she thought she could help her. We never talked about those magical summers when other family members were around.

I fell into her routine as if I had been born for it. I grew up going to the supermarket and did not realize anyone shopped daily for their food. Most mornings after breakfast, we would head to town with her wheeled wire shopping cart clanging behind us. She always saw someone she knew and exchanged greetings but didn't stop to chat. On rainy days we would take the trolley back to Lexington Avenue, but that was a rare treat.

We stopped at the green grocer for ripe fruit and vegetables. She had a small garden tucked behind the back hedges, and we would check that before our shopping trips. We crossed the street (she had a shopping order that did not coincide with the streetscape) for the corner delicatessen. She let me hold the tongs to fish a fat kosher pickle from the barrel, and I learned to quickly slide it into the waxy white bags that hung on the hook beside it.

Sunna introduced me to my first pickled tomato. At the bakery, they always greeted her by name, and she introduced me as her oldest granddaughter. Some days we would get a loaf of crusty rye bread with caraway seeds, and on others, onion rolls she used to make Sam's lunch.

One day a week, we went downtown just for fun. Sunna would purchase a bag of lemon drops in clear cellophane with blue stars and carefully unwrap them for us as we walked. She was an extraordinary knitter. I still have two sweaters she knit me with an intricate leaf pattern. I adore them. When she found out we were adopting a little boy, she knit him a blue sweater in a cable stitch pattern with whale buttons and a matching blanket. Dann wore that sweater on the long flight home, the blanket on our laps. I thought about her many times that night into day and back into night.

Carefully wrapped, I keep the sweater and blanket in a cedar chest in the attic. One day Dann will have a little one to wear that blue sweater.

We go to the yarn shop. Sometimes she buys wool or needles of bone or aluminum. Once, we brought in a dusky violet sweater she made for her sister Betty. The man who made button holes, she explained, would pick it up and return it the next week. Other times we'd look at the paper patterns, and she'd ask what styles I liked.

We went to The Fair, a department store in town, and she bought me a winter coat before I went back to start school. I do not remember exactly what the coat looked like, only that the store was fancy and had tri-fold mirrors on the third floor, and I was happy to try on a dozen coats and spin around.

During one of the summers I spent with her, we went to Rutherford to visit Sam's sister and brother-in-law. Sam's elderly father, my *Zayde,* lived with them, but he was scheduled to go to a nursing home the following week. Everyone was sad, and I was too young to understand why at the time.

Sunna, years later, explains that Annie (Sam's sister) loved her father and wanted to go back to being his daughter, not his nurse. I wrestle with that. Bob requires extra time and assistance with some daily tasks, but as I write, he does not need extraordinary medical care.

Dann reminds me that we can get help anytime I need it so that I can remain a wife. I know exactly what he means, and it is said with love. I just don't know yet what I'm going to do.

*William Carlos Williams has a way of threading through my life. He was a physician in Rutherford, New Jersey and one of my favorite poets. When our son first went to Montclair University, his residence hall was named William Carlos Williams. In one of my favorite films, *Paterson,* Adam Driver is a bus-driving poet who, along with his wife, finds love and wonder in ordinary things.

*"Grab the broom of anger and
drive off the beast of fear."*

– Zora Neale Hurston

April 2022
The Coals of Anger

*I wake up angry. Sometimes there is just no
place to put the anger. Yesterday I heard a
woman explain to her companion "that
everything happens for a reason." Luckily
(for her), I was a bystander and didn't make
a comment. Sometimes I wish I had that
kind of faith. You put your fate and that of
the ones you love in the hands of a higher
power. I know kind friends for whom that
gives both peace and fortitude. I am not one
of those people.*

Bob took early retirement a few years ago and used
to do the books for our small business. I am
managing that on my own now. The business is
mostly online, so we are the target of countless
organizations vying for our charity dollars. Many are
worthy, but we say no. We've thought long and hard
about where we donate, and for over twenty years,
it has been St Jude Children's Research Hospital. If

you don't understand why, please look them up. We donate monthly, and when our business does well, we give extra, quietly.

The parents of those young souls do not ask why their children have cancer. They already know there is no reason. They just know they have to fight. Sometimes that is not enough. I am irritated when I hear trite conversation. I wear my AirPods more and more. I sit with a mom who dreams of nothing more than sharing a popsicle at the playground with her daughter. I close my eyes and wish that for her one day soon.

The first time I read the words *rare sporadic progressive neurological disorder* in regards to Bob's disease, they take my breath away. Five words strung together that make some days seem hopeless, and the anger swells.

The anger masks fear and vulnerability. Ask any spouse or parent who has been given a diagnosis whether they are prepared for it or not. You cannot lose yourself in the grief for too long. There is too much to do and too much to learn.

There is always hope, whether you see it or not. Some diseases will be cured. Some will advance slowly, so you leave nothing unsaid. Sometimes it's better not to think of the future but just let each day unfold before you. It helps the anger fade away.

I will not dwell on how I presumed life would unfold, so I hone my strength and will myself to live in the present.

*"No matter how slow you swim,
you are still lapping everybody on the couch."*

—Author Unknown

June 1993
Just Swim

Bob and Dann were born to swim. From an early age, I could swim to save myself, but I did not learn that a long, smooth glide through the water would change my life until I was forty-nine.

When Dann was about two, Bob started taking him to the pool every Saturday in the summer. Occasionally I would tag along. On one particular day in late June, Bob put Dann on his back and told him to hold on. He did sea serpent motions in the water, diving deep and then rising high on the surface. Dann held on tight, but even more remarkable was that he instinctively knew when to hold his breath when Bob dove deep, let the air out when he rose to the surface, only to hold his breath again for the next plunge.

And just like that, after that day, Dann could swim. We used to spend weekday afternoons at the pool splashing with the other little ones, but now Dann wanted to spend all his time in the big pool. We taught him freestyle, and Bob helped him coordinate his stroke and kick with his breathing. During "adult" swim, he ran down to the fenced-in playground with his friends.

Over the years, Bob and Dann swam while I sat on the sidelines. Bob would swim in the morning before work. By age seven, Dann competed on a USS Swim Team and with our local summer swim club. He was a swim instructor and lifeguard, swam through school and coached the summer swim team. Bob, steady as a rock, swam indoors in winter and outdoors in summer.

When the JCC pool in Cherry Hill closed down to make way for town homes on the river, Bob went searching for a fitness club with a pool. One day, from the trainer's desk, he called me and asked if I wanted to join. I said yes. I didn't know if I would swim, but I said yes.

The first few months were challenging for me. I did not yet have precise nor well-timed breathing. My arms were not strong enough to glide smoothly, and I rotated from my shoulders instead of my core. The pool did not love me at first, but I loved it anyway. I kept at it.

Finally, one day, it all comes together, and I don't have to think about every little step. I find the wall and lift my feet behind me. I want to push off hard and glide. The streamline (I still hear Dann's coach yelling "streamline" from the deck) is my favorite part. In early summer, the outdoor pool we swim at is a very cold and long fifty meters. Every day when I finish that first lap, I celebrate and keep going.

Swimming is zen. It is silent meditation in a noisy world. I do my best thinking, praying and dreaming there. I work on problems and prose without interruption. A long black line, soft blue waves topped with morning sunlight and me.

When **MSA** robs Bob of his balance and he can no longer cycle, I say a grateful prayer that he can still swim. It's not like before, but with physical therapy and muscle memory, he perseveres. The alternative is untenable.

I follow the work of Dr. Joel Stager, Professor Emeritus in Kinesiology at Indiana University. He says, "Active swimmers appear to have greater cell density and connectedness in the cerebellum, which can improve gait and balance and help prevent falls." Make it so. Please make it so.

Except on vacation, Bob and I swim our laps at different times. Sometimes the pools are crowded, and lanes are at a premium, and we don't relish sharing. I let him go alone to continue the grace of independence. Should there ever come a time when he needs me to accompany him, my arm crooked so he can slip his in, I will be there.

*"I never paint dreams or nightmares.
I paint my own reality."*

– Frida Kahlo

April 2021
Bad Dreams

I wake up in a heart-pounding panic in the middle of the night. The clock in the cable box says 3:03 AM, and Henry, our dog, stirs at the foot of our bed. I can't take him out because the house alarm doesn't turn off for another two hours. Bob is sleeping soundly beside me.

I look out the window closest to Bob's side of the bed, and our neighbor's side porch light softly illuminates part of our backyard. Our motion lights have not been triggered, and the garage door is closed.

Now, I realize it is the panic of the every day. There is a pit in my stomach as I simultaneously make a list of all the things around the house I know nothing about and wonder how I am going to ask Bob how to do those things? If I just make a list and start asking questions, surely he will know I am planning for life without him, even if that may be years away.

To allay my fears, I decide to start small. Where is the main shut-off value for the water? We have five hose posts and sprinklers, and in the cellar, I don't know where you turn the water off and on for any of them. I assume they are spigots like outside, but some are not. Bob takes me to the basement a few days later and shows me a blue lever coming out of a copper pipe. I would never have guessed that lever was for hose water. It takes days to learn where all the levers are, but one day when Bob is in the shower, I take photos so I will remember for the next time. I hope next time is a long time from now.

There was a retired school nurse on our street who just loved Dann. She would watch him occasionally when we went out and bring him coloring books and stickers as she decluttered her home. Her husband, the former town fire chief, had been ill for a long time. When he died, Marge became frozen in time.

It's something I've noticed before, and it makes me sad. I vow never to let it happen to me. When Frank, the nurse's beloved husband, died, she didn't buy new clothes again. She drove the same car and sat on the same furniture. When something broke, she didn't want it fixed. You could tell by her surroundings what decade her husband died.

It isn't that I don't understand. I do. She had a life of beautiful memories, and they gave her comfort. She disengaged from activities where her friends would gather. Instead of living, she spent the next twenty years in the twilight of the past. Nothing we tried would change that.

"The fog comes. On little cat feet.
It sits looking. Over harbor and city.
On silent haunches.
And then moves on."

−Carl Sandburg

May 2022
Brain Fog

Bob does not often initiate a conversation. So, when he starts talking about being in a cloud, I put my book down and pay close attention.

"Can you describe it?" I gently ask.

He explains it to me, and I realize that it's both mental and physical. The mental part is that he knows what I am saying, but he doesn't always follow my point to the conclusion. The physical part is that he does not always see on the periphery, just what is right in front of him.

He says he feels comfortable at home and on our property, as well as at the pool, because he is familiar with those places. He can navigate them slowly. I think he may be saying this because he no longer wants to go anywhere and is now explaining why. I am painfully aware his decline started earlier than I realized.

"Is it like being in a fog?" I ask him. He nods. I wonder what precipitated the conversation, and I remembered yesterday I asked if he wanted me to call a friend of his he used to meet for lunch. I thought it might be nice if he came over for a visit.

He almost shouted. "No! He has his own problems. He doesn't need to know about mine."

I just say, "Okay."

While brain fog is not actually a medical condition, it can feel like a lack of mental clarity and impact the way a person feels about themselves. He tells me "the cloud" is in his head, that he always has a general feeling of fatigue. I can see that, especially after physical therapy, but I also see cognitive inefficiency. Bob reminds me it is just plain tiring to talk. I am not a medical professional, but I hope I can mitigate some of his behaviors by changing a few of my own.

I talk less. This is hard for me. I like to explain things. I do not like ambiguity. Still, I say less and less to compensate. I make it a point to talk to Dann most days as well as people in the neighborhood while I walk the dog. I have lots of email friends, some from an artist's group I used to run, some as far back as college. Many of us are loners, and the email is comforting.

Bob has been bowing his head when we watch television in the evening. For months, when I ask if he is okay, he says yes. But now, he explains, he doesn't want to see the commercials (they make it hard for him to follow the plot), *and* sometimes he has double vision at night. I know the latter is an MSA symptom. He likes me to choose the programs in the evening, so right after *Jeopardy,* he always hands me the remote.

Now I choose series or films on streaming services or PBS so that there are no commercials. I am not certain he is following the plot line, but he is calmer, and if either one of us talks about the storyline or takes a break, I pause the program midstream. Often the show triggers a memory from long ago.

These are small things to write about, but I have no big things to change. My mind flashes back to my mom in hospice. I had driven through the night to see her one last time and arrived at dawn. There was a door in her room that opened onto a lovely garden.

Outside the door, etched in a rock, was the Mother Teresa quote, "Not all of us can do great things. But we can do small things with great love."

"The practice of forgiveness is our most important contribution to the healing of the world."

–Marianne Williamson

January 1966
Boiling Over

By the time I was ten, I was often put in charge of my three younger siblings. It was a Saturday, and I don't know why my mother left us that clear, cold morning, but she did. We were watching TV when I smelled something burning. She had left two pots on the stove, and they were both bubbling over.

I have some jumbled memories that when my father would leave the house, my mom would leave in the other car shortly thereafter. Two things she would yell as she walked out the door were, "don't touch the stove" and "don't leave the house."

I ran into the kitchen, smoke filling the air. I should have turned off the burners, but my ten-year-old self heard mom's voice in her head. So, I told everyone to put on their slippers and grab their coats. We ran outside to wait for my mom to come back.

She saw us huddling on the porch as she pulled into the driveway, a short ten minutes later, our frozen breath hovering in the air. She brushed past us. The smell was acrid, even from outside. We followed her in, but did not enter the kitchen. She

71

turned off the burners, opened the windows and spent the rest of the day scraping food off the stove. My mother didn't say a word to me until the next morning.

Over the years, I replayed that scene in my head many times. I should have turned the burners off. I should have taken the kids to a neighbor. I'm never going to have kids. I'm never going to leave my kids alone. And later, I'm never going to make my son feel small because *I* have troubles.

I've done really silly things. When Dann first went to school, he would not eat sandwiches. So, I would cube leftover chicken or turkey along with some cheddar cheese for his lunch. I saved (and the neighbors saved for me) old margarine tubs because he would invariably throw the containers away.

When I picked him up from school one afternoon and asked how his day went, he said, "You packed me butter for lunch, Mom!"

Once home, I went to the refrigerator and found a neatly packed tub of turkey and cheese. Sure enough, I sent him to school with a full tub of margarine. I love how that kid threw his head back when he laughed.

I have not been a perfect mother, but I have always led with love. I remember when members of our extended family were repeatedly unkind in a situation I thought could easily be understood with a little more kindness.

Bob knew I could do nothing to fix it, hard as I tried and simply said, "Dann will grow up to be a fine man. You need not say another word or do another thing."

He did.

Jedidiah Jenkins in *Like Streams to the Ocean* relays a sentiment a pastor told him years ago: "Even if we don't know what's coming, we were made for it."

*"Nothing behind me, everything ahead
of me, as is ever so on the road."*

–Jack Kerouac

May 2022
The Yellow Brick Road

Some of the sidewalks in Haddonfield, New Jersey
are paved with long yellow brick. I do not know how
old they are, but in October 1682, Francis Collins, an
English Quaker and a bricklayer by trade, became
the first settler within the boundaries of what today is
Haddonfield. The sidewalks gently undulate, unlike
concrete, so you have to be very careful where you
walk.

After Bob settles into the physical therapy waiting
room, I kiss his forehead and head out on my walk.
I go no matter the weather. As I round the second
corner, the *Wizard of Oz* song gets stuck in my head.
Old neighborhoods are as interesting to me as
mountain tops and this one, with swaths of yellow
brick, is no exception. Follow the yellow brick road, I
hum.

No need for music, the symphony of birds and
tree trimmers, the whoosh of lawn sprinklers is
enough. I am reminded of one of my favorite tales.

There are two men sitting on a bench. A small stack of yellow bricks is beside them. The first man says, "Let's have a contest to see who can throw a brick the highest." The second man agrees. The first man throws the brick straight up in the air. The second man says, "I can throw higher than that." He does. The first man asks for one more chance. He hurls the brick up in the air, and it never comes down.

There are two women talking on an airplane. After some time passes, one of the women closes her eyes and falls asleep. The other woman casually stares out the window. In the distance, she can see a large bird, and as it flies by, she sees something in its mouth. It is a yellow brick.

I look at my watch, and it is time to head back to the Physical Therapy office and meet Bob. He is putting his jacket on when I arrive and has papers filled with home exercises for the coming days. When we get to the car, we just sit for a moment. I tell him about the great walk I have just had and that it will be fun for us to walk there this summer when therapy is over. He smiles but doesn't answer.

*"Courage is not the absence of fear,
but rather the assessment that something
else is more important than fear."*

–Franklin Delano Roosevelt

April 1992
Resilience

The long story of how we became a family really belongs to Dann. We agreed to share some of the tale, and for a few seasons before he started school, I was invited to talk to prospective adoptive families at the Pearl S. Buck Foundation. In those five days in Central America, the way I lived my life profoundly changed. In all the days after, it did not matter what happened before. Resilience coursed through my veins. You can decide if it was bravery or courage or the hand of a higher power. I just knew I was called to do this.

I learn that you can hold two disparate feelings simultaneously for days on end. I could hold my breath as we walked through throngs of people into the courtyard of the US Embassy, the top three floors blown off by war. At the same time, my heart would melt as my new son's small fingers would curl around mine.

We would drive to the airport in the dark of night in a taxi with no instrument panel, sounds of the army right beside us, marching along the unlit highway. Then, I would look over, our son nestled in Bob's arms playing with a ring of plastic keys.

As the sun rises, our plane finally lifts off for home, the aroma of coffee in the air. We have been on the precipice of joy for five days and have finally gone over the edge.

You must decide to be brave. You must choose it on the days fear envelops you like the fog. The fog signals that change is coming. If you don't push through now, you will miss the real life you were meant to live.

Until the paper crumbles, I carry this quote by Brene Brown in my pocket, *"Sometimes the bravest and most important thing you can do is just show up."*

The parallels between my son's arrival and my husband's health challenges are strikingly similar. While I understand that curiosity is innate, not every question requires an answer. And if and when you do answer questions, remember the people you love are listening to what you say and listening to how you answer. They are all that matters.

"Sorrow is so easy to express and yet so hard to tell."

—Joni Mitchell

January 2022
Observation

Before we have a name for Bob's challenges, I start looking at websites designed to assist and offer information to loved ones who have slipped into the roles of care partners seemingly overnight.

One day you are planning a vacation or looking forward to a milestone anniversary.

Next, you find yourself on websites with walkers and grab bars while you ask silently, "Is this really happening to us?"

Hope and despair are just different sides of the same coin. I see that acutely now.

I have never been good at small talk, nor at sharing personal information, whether they be strangers on a plane or acquaintances. I used to get quite uncomfortable before I was required to attend gatherings for either Bob's job or mine. He always seemed at ease.

One day he calmly told me to be an anthropologist, just slip into the role of "the watcher." I had good success at being a non-participant observer. Oh, how hard some people could *work* a room.

I find myself in that position once again. There are few people with whom I share our personal stories, even fewer that I would chime in with when they are talking about health. Some find comfort in the camaraderie. I do not. Still, I listen.

You may wonder how then I could write this book. I do it from arm's length, without comment or interaction except from my editor, a friend and my son. It's the way I weave all the discordant elements in my mind when so little makes sense.

It is humbling to be in uncharted waters, and I often think of my paternal grandmother Jeanne. She was one of the first patients to undergo a heart valve replacement by the renowned surgeon Michael Debakey. They became lifelong friends. Her husband, my Grandpa Dave, a pharmacist who owned a corner drug store, and Debakey's father the same.

Jeanne moved slowly, never explained it was due to her health and was always the epitome of grace. She had a nurturing and forgiving heart and taught me to always look for the good in people. Without saying a word, how to listen more than I talked and give more than I had.

She would want me to find my people, a tribe of kindred spirits to help me navigate. I know many have walked these steps before me, and I promise her I will find them.

"Ring the bells that still can ring. Forget your perfect offering. There is a crack in everything. That's how the light gets in."

–Anthem by Leonard Cohen

April 2022
From Darkness

We have a small greenhouse where perennial herbs winter over, and I start seedlings to protect them from the dipping temperatures in early spring. It is barely light out when I head out back. The grass beneath my feet crunches with frost.

The pane on the lower left, closest to the rail fence, has a small crack in the glass. I should tape it over, I think, but just then, the morning sun shines on the greenhouse, and the light passes through that crack in a way that seems to be a sign.

Signs are everywhere, but it is freezing outside, and after I am certain that the tomatoes and cucumbers, mint and oregano have survived, I run into the house to brew a pot of coffee.

When I finally relax with the steaming mug in my hand, I recall the repeating stanza of "Anthem," *the redeeming acceptance of light illuminating the darkness*, compassion and love overcoming pain, brushing against acceptance, but not quite ready for what comes next.

If you or a loved one are startled by a life-changing diagnosis with the possibility of remission, you make a plan. Even if the road will be long and winding, you see the light at the end of the tunnel. It is what will keep you going during your darkest days.

Bob's prognosis is not optimistic. It is a hard morning for me. I have pride in figuring out solutions to difficult problems, but this is different. Dr. Z's words echo loudly in my head, "There is no cure. There is only symptomatic treatment that wanes over time." I know this is true, and yet inside, I am fighting the truth with everything I have.

On my way up to the studio, I am still thinking about Leonard Cohen. I know there are lyrics to comfort and look them up before I begin to work.

> *"The light is the capacity to reconcile your experience, your sorrow, with every day that dawns. It is that understanding that is beyond significance or meaning that allows you to live a life and embrace the disasters and sorrows and joys that are our common lot. I think all other visions are doomed to irretrievable gloom. And whenever anyone asks us to accept a perfect solution, that should immediately alert us to the flaws in that presentation."*

I finish reading and walk back downstairs to give Bob a hug. He is wrapped in a quilt watching the Science Channel. He smiles, and I head back up to work.

"It isn't the mountains ahead to climb that wear you out; it's the pebble in your shoe."

-Muhammad Ali

May 2022
On Being an Athlete

Finally, after a COVID hiatus, the Broad Street Run is scheduled, although spectators are discouraged. It is a glorious day to run. Since he moved to Philadelphia, Dann has embraced all the city has to offer, and the run is no exception.

Before Dann was born, I would accompany Bob to bicycle races. Sometimes they were time trials or road races where I'd see him only at the beginning and at the end. Other times the races were loops through the rain and the mud, and once in the snow! I'd warm my hands and feet in the car while I waited to cheer him on at the next loop.

When he was young, Dann played T-ball and soccer. We were the quiet parents, watching him try different things until he figured out where he belonged and what he loved. Sometimes the most fun was the pizza afterward.

In all the years of all the sports, this is the first time I recall being a homebound spectator. Besides countless swimming and track events, Bob and I have cheered Dann in two Asbury Park triathlons (open water is a heartstopper), others in North Jersey and Philadelphia. He was always proud and delighted to have us there.

In the days before the race, he is chatting with friends, new and old, about the ten-mile race on the longest street in the world. In addition to his running club, after work, he goes on training runs with his friend, Steven. He sends me the routes they've traversed from his phone.

On those days after dinner, I sit with Bob and show him the routes. We know Philadelphia so well, and it is special to see Dann enjoying those same places. Now and then, I'll tell a story about the River Drive or the Ben Franklin Bridge, hoping Bob will contribute to the memories. He is proud of Dann, but doesn't say much.

On race morning, I say a prayer for all the runners and set the DVR. Dann sends race tracker info to my phone. I watch some of the race on TV and see his friend Katelyn. Later I see a little video of Dann and Steven. I know they are going to have a wonderful day and head out to work in the garden.

When I return, we have fresh dill, kale, and baby lettuce for lunch. Bob says he will sit and watch the run with me. We are not really sport "watchers," except perhaps for the Tour de France and the Olympics, but Bob knows it's important to me.

An hour later, Dann texts: *SUCCESS*.

He phones me after he gets off the subway and is excited and feels great. He's going to shower and then meet his running friends for brunch. My heart is full.

TREADING WATER

I'm not sure what to say to Bob, but I know he is struggling with no longer being an athlete. I sat quietly beside him, wondering if he'll say more. He does. He tells me that he didn't know when he stopped riding his bike two years ago that would be the last time. My heart hurts. I have no frame of reference for the perseverance and fortitude it takes to be a lifelong athlete. How can I help him with this?

Bob is a *one-foot-in-front-of-the-other* type of guy, so he does not lament for long. I am also painfully aware his health challenges have robbed him of deep emotion. Perhaps that is a blessing. I ask him if he would be interested in a recumbent bicycle since the center of gravity is low and doesn't require the same sort of balance.

I tell him, "I'll ride alongside you in the park."

He shakes his head no, but I make a note to revisit this topic again. Maybe he will think about it.

"The marvelous thing about a good question is that it shapes our identity as much by the asking as it does by the answering."

–David Whyte

May 2022
Lifelong Learners
Part 1

When my son was in graduate school, he began to refer to himself as a lifelong learner. The shift in his quest for knowledge was contagious and continues to this day. I had often heard the term when retirees went back to the classroom or workshop to learn new skills. It is gratifying to see it cross the generations.

Not always an excellent "classroom" student, especially in university-required courses, I found that reading and learning new things in other ways became a big part of my life. Dann had a summer swimming friend, Allie, who reminded me of myself. We both read fiction and nonfiction books simultaneously and shared a penchant for the chocolate outside of Oreo cookies but eschewed the creme in the middle.

When Bob's health started to decline, I stopped reading fiction and used that time to better understand his illness. I poured over PubMed abstracts of **MSA-C,** the type of **Multiple System Atrophy** his neurologists have assigned to him. At last count, there were 1,492 (the year Columbus sailed the ocean blue) papers, and I will never read them all.

I am unfamiliar with medical terminology, so as I previously noted, I keep a medical dictionary tab open on my laptop to plow through the research. I have come to the conclusion, after reading many abstracts, that the knowledge of the molecular pathogenesis of this devastating disease is still incomplete, but "updated consensus criteria and combined fluid and imaging biomarkers have increased its diagnostic accuracy." I am not sure how that is helpful or if any meaningful research will occur because of these discoveries.

I also followed a promising clinical trial of Verdiperstat (Biohaven). It was a first-in-class brain penetrant, irreversible MPO enzyme inhibitor. After three years of a double-blind, placebo-controlled parallel-group study, it was determined to be ineffective.

One morning I picked my laptop up to read the next abstract and then gently put it down. I am armed with the mechanics, prognosis and lack of research on this disease and will read no more. In the back of my mind, though, something is brewing.

I decide to go for a walk. A long walk.

"A man who carries a cat by the tail learns something he can learn in no other way."

— *Mark Twain*

May 2022
Lifelong Learners
Part 2

We are enjoying beautiful spring weather in the garden state, and I spend a lot of time outdoors. Right outside our front door are azaleas in various hues of pink and a Chinese wisteria with long racemes in showy purple and white. Our Craftsman bungalow was built c. 1918, and we have taken care to plant perennials of the era instead of modern hybrids.

Further down our cobblestone paths are columbine, hostas, and two hydrangeas that symbolize gratitude and grace are just starting to leaf. Our neighbor Walter, who lived until he was 101, gifted us a redwood seedling from his majestic mother tree. He told Bob he brought the two redwood trees in his yard back from the Himalayas in the mid-1950s.

On the far side of our property, we have a long stand of bamboo that shields us from the main road. It has grown more than 300 feet in length since Bob and Dann planted it about twenty years ago.

By the time I turn the corner and our home is out of sight, my spirits soar. I pick up my pace and head toward the park. There are saws buzzing and a loud construction crew building a patio. I am glad I remembered to tuck my AirPods in my pocket. I don't listen to music on my walks, but I always have a podcast cued up just in case.

I have eclectic listening habits. If I listen to an interesting guest on one of my favorite podcasts, I will seek them out on others. For almost ten years, I have listened to Rich Roll, who defies characterization. He is an accomplished yet humble man. I am drawn to the insightful and thought-provoking questions he asks his guests. Each guest provides a diverse experience that enriches the airwaves.

I was privileged to find Dr. Andrew Huberman on Rich's podcast and subsequently devoured episodes of his own podcast, the magnificent, *The Huberman Lab*. I do not have a science background, and now I am beginning to understand the complexities of the human body.

Dr. Huberman is a neuroscientist and explains how the brain works with other organs to control our health, behaviors and perceptions. I am not only grateful that he spells the words he uses but offers a framework of scientific nomenclature so the listener can not only comprehend each episode but put it to practical use.

One evening while ruminating about a particularly interesting podcast with Dr. Rhonda Patrick, I had an aha moment.

TREADING WATER

I review my copious notes from *The Huberman Lab* and the PubMed articles I've read about **MSA-C**. Armed with both questions and more information, I remember a specific abstract I bookmarked and read this line over and over: "The pathogenesis of **MSA-C** is characterized by propagation of misfolded α-synuclein from neurons to oligodendroglia and cell-to-cell spreading in a 'prion-like' manner, oxidative stress, proteasomal and mitochondrial dysfunction and dysregulation of myelin lipids." I read the definitions of these words over and over until I comprehend each one.

My rudimentary science brain is brimming with ideas. What if I gave Bob EPA and DHA, which are long-chain omega-3 polyunsaturated fatty acids? I already take these in marine algae form. He could use fish oil. Since the myelin sheath, I have learned, is mostly made of fat, I could increase healthy fats in Bob's diet, and perhaps his nerve cells could communicate more effectively and finally, increase his protein intake to support amino acids like glutathione that protect the mitochondria.

There are countless anecdotal stories of how quality nutrition and supplements heal health challenges when conventional medicine does not work. Whether they are accurate or not, I do not know. Discoveries come from places heretofore unimagined. So, I open my heart should a miracle come our way.

> *"Imagination will often carry us to worlds that never were. But without it we go nowhere."*
>
> *– Carl Sagan*

May 2022
Between Darkness and Light

I am still half asleep as the rising sun peeks through the wooden blinds in our bedroom. I hear the screen door bang against the storm door in the back of the house. *Bob is home from his morning ride*, I think. I have always said a small prayer of thanks every time Bob rides and returns safely home. I sit up with a jolt when I realize that Bob can no longer ride.

I slide back under the covers to *will it so.* I want to close my eyes so tightly that I am transported back in time. I have willed for my grandma not to die and for a new dress to wear to the seventh-grade dance. It never works, but I tell myself I will be okay because there is still time to figure things out.

I get out of bed and make my way to the living room, where Bob is sitting on the couch drinking coffee. "The pool is closed for maintenance," he says. "Did I wake you?"

It is one of those beautiful clear mornings, not a cloud in the sky. I pour a cup of coffee and make us some toast from whole wheat sourdough bread I purchased at the farmer's market this past Saturday. It smells like honey.

Today is the last day of Bob's scheduled physical therapy, and he slowly rises to get ready. Routine frames Bob's day, so I am already thinking about how to fill the space on Monday and Thursday therapy has occupied.

His therapist is always upbeat, complementing Bob's progress, encouraging him to keep up with the routine on a twice-daily basis. He treats Bob with respect and encourages him to call if he ever has questions. The office manager, who always greets us by name, bids us farewell and we make our way to the car.

I have preordered lunch from Maria's in Collingswood. We drive down the avenue, and luckily, there is parking nearby. I run in to pick up the sandwiches and drive the few blocks to the park near our house. We settle on a bench under mighty oaks that provide dappled sunlight, the little red bridge in the distance and unwrap our sandwiches.

*"Take care of all your memories.
For you cannot relive them."*

–Bob Dylan

April 1988
Driving to Florida

Bob and I have vacation time available and decide at the last minute to drive to Florida. We didn't even consider flying there. Our families remind us that this type of trip requires planning. We thank them for the advice, and while Bob fills the car with gas and checks the oil and tires, I pack two backpacks with shorts, swimsuits and goggles.

At the last minute, I run back into the house and grab towels and a beach blanket. On the way out of town, we stop at the grocery and fill our cooler with ice and snacks. We have no cell phones. There is no internet. We have one map of the Eastern Seaboard, and I ask Bob if he knows the way.

"South," he says, and we laugh as we travel down the highway.

When we are south of Washington DC and the rolling hills of Virginia, peppered with pink and white dogwoods, I offer to drive. Bob settles in for a long nap, and I cross into the Carolinas by early evening. We stop at a little roadside cafe for dinner and to stretch our legs. Behind the cafe are colorful painted

95

picnic tables, and the friendly waitress tells us we can get our food "to go" and eat outside.

I can't remember exactly what we ordered, but I do know we had hush puppies. We have them rarely, but somehow they find their way into the best times of our lives. When we eloped, Bob took me to a little joint on the way to our honeymoon, and they served the most delicious hush puppies. Until today.

We take a walk around the grounds. The family who runs the cafe lives behind it, and we see kids on a tire swing next to a small clapboard white house. By the time we hit the Georgia state line, it's clear we will not be awake enough to drive straight through to Florida. There are no vacancies at any motels we pass for the next two hours. Finally Bob pulls into a scary-looking Bates-type motel with a vacancy sign. We pay cash for the room and flop on the bed, fully dressed.

Around 3:00 AM, a group of bikers enters the parking lot, engines revving, and they go around and around in circles. Their headlights illuminate our room at every turn. I hear a bottle break. My heart is pounding, and I am scared. There is nothing to do but wait until morning.

About an hour later, there is a knock at our door. I don't want to answer it, but we know that door could easily be busted down, so we do.

On the other side is a biker with our room key in his hand. "Ma'am," he says, "you left your key in the door. That's not safe." He smiles. I take the key, thank him, and wait for the morning sun.

TREADING WATER

The rest of the trip was pleasant and uneventful. We travel to the ocean and Cape Canaveral and explore the wildlife on Merritt Island. I remember Willa Cather's words as we traverse the state, *"the end is nothing, the road is all."*

Epilogue

*"Time is very slow for those who wait. Very fast
for those who are scared. Very long for those
who lament. Very short for those who celebrate.
But for those who love, time is eternal."*

—*William Shakespeare*

Today is our fortieth wedding anniversary, and it
seems a fitting time to end this book. It is a hot, still
summer day, much like the day we got married.
Much like that day, our lives have changed in ways
unimagined.

We abandoned our plans for a big wedding right
in the middle of choosing the flowers and the cake.
There was family drama over religious differences
and divorces and who would marry us. We did not
thrive on chaos and pulled back from our families.
We were in love and decided to elope.

Bob and I were married by the mayor of a small
town in Pennsylvania on a Friday evening in the
middle of summer. We headed west, and that's how
we ended up at that little joint that served hush
puppies. We sat amidst noisy, laughing families in

shorts, Bob in a suit, me in a short white dress with silver sandals, and we had the time of our lives.

So, again there will be no big party I had planned, it's just not necessary anymore. Less than an hour away, I found a little place on the outskirts of the Pine Barrens that serves hush puppies. On the way back we will stop for ice cream and water ice at Dippy's, the quintessential ice cream drive-in and then head for home.

Acknowledgments

Thank you, dear reader, for trusting me to tell my story when you have your own. What comforts me may be different for you. There are as many ways to walk through our challenges as there are stars in the sky.

Live for those who are having trouble taking those steps themselves. Live for yourself every single day, for the days are only borrowed.

Sometimes it is the smallest fork in the road that leads you to a completely different life and makes you realize how long you have been standing still. Wherever Bob's crisis of health leads us, we will go.

Made in the USA
Middletown, DE
11 July 2022

69016008R00066